GOD'S PROVISION
FOR YOU

Printed in China

ISBN 978-1-951701-39-0

Created and assembled for Joel Osteen Ministries by Breakfast for Seven
2150 E. Continental Blvd., Southlake, TX 76092
breakfastforseven.com

GOD'S PROVISION
for You

JOEL OSTEEN

INTRODUCTION

"Whoever believes in me, as Scripture has said, rivers of living water will flow from within them."
John 7:38, NIV

Friend,

Have you ever heard someone say, "I'll believe it when I see it"? Maybe you have said that yourself. But let me encourage you to turn it around today: You've got to believe God before you'll "see" and experience the *"rivers of living water"* which Jesus speaks of in John 7:38.

That's what faith is all about, and it's why I wrote this book. Every morning when we wake up, the first thing we should say is, *"Lord, thank You for Your goodness. Thank You for the breakthrough, the healing, the provision."* As you do, I believe you will rise to a new level of faith, letting go of the old, ready to receive the new things He has for you.

I realize it's not always easy, especially when things aren't going our way. The world often tries to make us feel like victims. But we are victors in Christ Jesus. So, we have to rise to the occasion each and every day, shake off what didn't work out, and declare, "I am choosing to believe that I am blessed!"

Can I tell you? That is exactly how God sees you: He calls you blessed, anointed, empowered, and equipped. The key is to see yourself as your Creator God does. The more you do, the more you are going to see the overflowing blessings and provision He has already prepared for you.

Let me pray this prayer over you:

Lord, thank You for leading my friend to these pages and allowing me to bless them with my words. Thank You for showing out in ways that they know it is Your hand on their life, and for making things happen that they couldn't make happen. Thank You for bringing out their gifts and talents in new ways. Lord, shower them with Your goodness and cause them to flourish underneath the abundance of Your overflow! In Jesus' name, amen."

CONTENTS

CHAPTER 1

YOUR PREPARED
Blessing

"No eye has seen, no ear has heard, and no mind has imagined what God has prepared for those who love him."

1 Corinthians 2:9, NLT

When God laid out the plan for your life, He lined up the right people, the right breaks, the right opportunities. He has blessings with your name on them. There's promotion, contracts, a business, a spouse, healing, restoration. He has already destined them to be yours. If you'll stay in faith and keep honoring God, at the right time you'll come in to what already belongs to you. It's a prepared blessing.

That's what happened with Adam and Eve.

In the book of Genesis, it talks about how in the first five days, God created the heavens, earth, sky, land, and water. When He finished the big things, He didn't stop there. He got down to the small things — the details. He planted a garden, put beautiful flowers in it, and luscious fruit. He designed rivers to flow through it. He put precious treasures in the ground — onyx, gold, silver. He went to great lengths to make sure it was exactly what He wanted, down to the smallest details. When He finally finished it and put the last touches on this magnificent garden, the Scripture says He took Adam, whom He had just breathed life into, and put Him in the garden.

Notice how Adam came in to a prepared blessing — something that God had already finished for him. He didn't get there and have to work night and day, constantly struggling, thinking, "How am I going to survive?" There were fruit trees all around, crystal clear water flowing right before him, provision everywhere he looked. He didn't live worried, thinking, "I've got food. I've got water, but how am I going to make a living? How am I going to provide for my family?" There were resources at his disposal. Everything he needed to live a victorious, abundant life was right there in the garden. God had specifically prepared it for him. In the same way, God has some prepared blessings in store for you. He's working behind the scenes right now, arranging things in your favor, getting it all perfectly in place. At the right time, He's going to bring you into your garden, into what He's already finished. You couldn't have made it happen on your own. You didn't deserve it. You didn't earn it. It's just the goodness of God bringing you into a prepared blessing.

Falling into Place

A friend of mine came from a large family that had emigrated from another country. They were very poor, and nobody had made much of their life. They had a defeated mindset. My friend started coming to Lakewood and hearing about how he was a victor and not a victim, and how he could rise up and set a new standard for his family. One day, a friend told him about a job cleaning equipment at the medical center. He interviewed and got the job. He was working the graveyard shift.

Every once in a while, they would have procedures at night. He would watch the technicians and study how they did it. At one point, one of the technicians took another job. The supervisor had seen this man's dedication, and even though my friend didn't have formal training, they promoted him and gave him that job. He became an assistant technician. He kept being faithful. A couple of years later, the main technician left, and they put this man in charge of the whole department. A few years went by and he began to think, "If I could buy this piece of equipment, I could do this on my own and travel from hospital to hospital." Playing basketball one afternoon, he met a man that had a banking business. He shared his dream of starting his own company. The man said, "I like you. Come by my bank, and we'll loan you the money." Things kept falling into place. Today he owns a very large, successful company. They're one of the leaders in the field.

What happened? My friend came in to a prepared blessing. God had been working on his garden, lining up the right people, giving him good breaks, causing him to be at the right place. At one point,

"If you'll stay in faith and keep honoring God, at the right time you'll come in to what already belongs to you. It's a prepared blessing."

Joel

after years of being faithful, God said, "All right, your garden is done. Now I'm going to bring you in to what I've prepared for you — a good land, not where you're cleaning the equipment, but where you own the equipment, not where you have to work for the company, but where you run the company."

Worth Waiting For

When I was twenty-two years old, I walked into a jewelry store and met Victoria for the first time. You know what she was? A prepared blessing. I looked up and said, "God, You did good." In a big city like Houston, there are thousands of jewelry stores that I could have gone into. But God controls the whole universe. He knows how to bring you into your garden. He said, in effect, "Joel, I've got something finished for you. You've stayed in faith; now I've got a prepared blessing that I'm ready to bring you into." God directed my steps. I met Victoria that day, and my life has never been the same.

Maybe you're thinking, "Well, Joel, I've been single so long. I don't think I'll ever meet the right person." No, there's a husband, a wife that has your name on them. God's getting it all prepared. At the right time, God will say, "All right, I'm done. Here's what I've been working on." You'll meet the person of your dreams. You'll say, like I did, "God, that was worth waiting for. You outdid Yourself." Don't get discouraged. You may not see anything happening, but God is at work, getting your garden prepared. When He's finished, He's going to bring you into it.

Stored-up Blessings

God's dream for your life is to bring you into a garden of abundance — a garden filled with favor, opportunity, good health, great relationships. You may not be there yet, but don't worry, your garden is on the way. Psalm 31:19, NLT says, ***"How great is the goodness you have stored up for those who fear you. You lavish it on those who come to you for protection, blessing them before the watching world."***

There are businesses stored up that God is about to release. There is promotion stored up, and it has your name on it. There's a new house stored up, a baby stored up, a husband stored up, healing stored up. Because you love the Lord, God is about to release what He has prepared for you. Because you honor God, because you're faithful, you're not going to have to go find the blessings, the blessings are going to find you. Something is tracking you down right now — not defeat, not lack, not self-pity. No, favor is looking for you. Promotion is looking for you. Healing is looking for you. You're about to come in to your garden, into a prepared blessing — something that you've never seen!

How great is the
goodness you have
stored up for those who
fear you. You lavish it
on those who come
to you for protection,
blessing them before the
watching world.

Psalm 31:19, NLT

Faith Reflection

What are you believing God for? Maybe you've been praying, trusting Him, but it's taking longer than you thought. Too often, we look at our circumstances and come up with excuses as to why it's not going to happen. No, God is not limited by our circumstances, by what family we come from, by who's against us. He has every intention of bringing you into the garden He has prepared for you. God has the final say.

"Don't get discouraged.
You may not see anything
happening, but God is
at work, getting your
garden prepared. When
He's finished, He's going
to bring you into it."

Joel

CHAPTER 2

THINK POWER
Thoughts

"Be careful what you think, because your thoughts run your life."

Proverbs 4:23, NCV

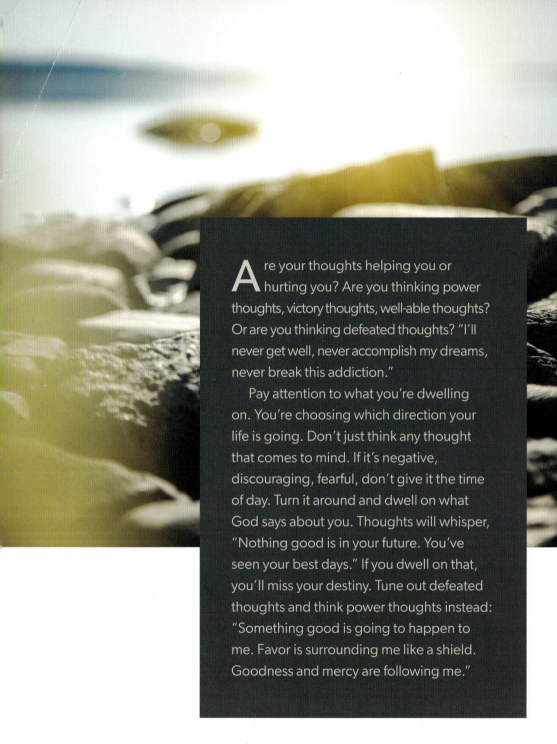

Are your thoughts helping you or hurting you? Are you thinking power thoughts, victory thoughts, well-able thoughts? Or are you thinking defeated thoughts? "I'll never get well, never accomplish my dreams, never break this addiction."

Pay attention to what you're dwelling on. You're choosing which direction your life is going. Don't just think any thought that comes to mind. If it's negative, discouraging, fearful, don't give it the time of day. Turn it around and dwell on what God says about you. Thoughts will whisper, "Nothing good is in your future. You've seen your best days." If you dwell on that, you'll miss your destiny. Tune out defeated thoughts and think power thoughts instead: "Something good is going to happen to me. Favor is surrounding me like a shield. Goodness and mercy are following me."

Power Up Your Thinking

When you're in tough times, the enemy will work overtime trying to convince you that the problem is too big, that you'll never get out of debt, that your child will never turn around. He knows if he can keep you defeated in your thoughts, then he can keep you defeated in your life. The battle is taking place in our minds. When thoughts tell you that it's never going to change, that you can't take it anymore, that you should just give up on your dream, that's when you turn it around and think power thoughts. Thinking weak thoughts only draws in more weakness. Instead, start declaring courage, start declaring strength: "Yes, this problem is big, but I've been armed with strength for every battle. I am full of can-do power. What God started in my life, He will finish. This difficulty didn't come to stay; it came to pass."

God said He will never let you face anything that you can't handle. He will always give you the grace, the strength, the faith for what comes your way. But if you're believing the lies that it's too much, then you're dwelling on weak, limiting, can't-do-it thoughts. You're going to feel overwhelmed, and you'll get stuck where you are. Pay attention to what's going on in your mind.

This is what happened to the Israelites. Moses sent twelve men to spy out the Promised Land. After forty days, ten came back and said, "Moses, we'll never defeat them. The people are huge. They look like giants. We don't have a chance." God had already promised them the victory. He had already said that was their land, but notice what they were thinking: weak, defeated, limiting, fearful thoughts. The other two spies, Joshua and Caleb, came back with a different report. They said, "Moses, we are well-able. Yes the people are big, but we know our God is bigger. Let us go in at once and take the land." What's interesting is, Joshua and Caleb saw the same giants as the other ten spies. They saw the same problem, the same opposition, the same land, but instead of thinking defeated thoughts, they chose to think power thoughts. Joshua and Caleb weren't any bigger than the other spies. They didn't have more training, more experience, more weapons. The only difference was their thinking.

Guard Your Mind

The negative report from the ten spies began to spread throughout the Israelites' camp. Before long, the people were afraid, worried. They said, "Moses, let's go back to Egypt. Let's go back to being slaves." That's how powerful our thoughts are. Ten men infected the rest of the people. The Israelites ended up wandering in the desert for forty years. Be careful how you think. Don't get infected and miss your destiny. Are you like one of the ten spies? "I can't beat this illness, I can't accomplish my dream, I don't have the connections. This is not going to work; it's going to ruin my business." None of this is a surprise to God. You wouldn't be facing it if you couldn't handle it. Like the Israelites, He's already promised you the victory.

The Scripture says, *"But thanks be to God, who always causes us to triumph in Christ . . ."* (2 Corinthians 2:14, EHV). Not some of the time, not most of the time, but all of the time. It may be tough now, but keep the right perspective; victory is in your future. Healing is in your future, abundance is in your future, freedom is in your future. The giants may be big, but our God is bigger. The obstacle may be

"Be careful how you think. Don't get infected and miss your destiny. Are you like one of the ten spies?"

Joel

high, but our God is the Most High. I'm asking you to be a Joshua, be a Caleb. Think power thoughts, think can-do thoughts, think victory thoughts. Don't look at how big your problem is; look at how big your God is! He parted the Red Sea. He closed the mouths of lions. He brought the dead back to life. That obstacle in front of you is no match for Him. He didn't bring you this far to leave you. When you believe, all things are possible. Get your thoughts going in the right direction.

Don't Think Like Everyone Else

Isaiah 59:19 says, *"When the enemy comes in like a flood, The Spirit of the LORD will lift up a standard against him"* (NKJV). You're not fighting this battle on your own. The most powerful force in the universe is fighting for you, pushing back forces of darkness, keeping that sickness from taking you out, moving the wrong people out of the way, opening doors that no man can shut. All through the day, "I am well able. I have can-do power. I will overcome this obstacle. I will defeat this sickness. I will rise out of lack and struggle. I will accomplish my dreams." When you think like that, the Creator of the Universe goes to work, and miracles are set in motion.

It's significant that ten spies were negative and two were positive. It's about the same today. Eighty percent of people will be negative; twenty percent will be positive. Eighty percent will focus on how big the problem is, live afraid, tell you how you won't get well, how you should just settle where you are. If you're going to fulfill your destiny, you have to go against the grain. You can't just fit in and be afraid like everyone else, complain like the other coworkers, be negative like that neighbor. God is looking for Joshuas. He's looking for Calebs — people who stand out, people who believe when it seems impossible, people who aren't discouraged by how big the opposition is.

If this is going to happen, you have to guard your mind because negative news spreads faster than good news. Joshua and Caleb said we are well able. That news didn't go anywhere. When people heard the giants were too big, that they didn't have a chance, that news spread like wildfire throughout the camp. Negative thinking Is contagious. All around us there's negative news: how bad the sickness is, how bad the economy is. Analysts are telling us what could happen and how it may get much worse. I'm not faulting them. They're doing their job. It's good to be informed, but you can't let that poison stay in your spirit. If you keep dwelling on that, then you're going to end up afraid, worried, panicked, thinking you're not going to make it. When you think like that, it's a negative cycle that keeps drawing in more fear, more worry, more defeat.

"Don't call everything a conspiracy, like they do, and don't live in dread of what frightens them. Make the Lord of Heaven's Armies holy in your life. He is the one you should fear. He is the one who should make you tremble. He will keep you safe." (See Isaiah 8:11–14) You don't have to fear what the economy is going to do, fear the future. Just keep honoring God and He will keep you safe. He'll defeat your enemies, He'll do what medicine can't do, He'll turn your child around, He'll free you from that addiction.

This passage is saying not to think like everyone else. Don't think like the ten spies. When the majority is afraid, worried, negative,

you have to be on the offensive and say, "No, I'm not falling in to that trap. I'm not going to think weak, defeated thoughts. I'm going to think power thoughts. I know my God is still on the throne. I know Him being for me is more than the world being against me. I am well-able to accomplish my dream. I will defeat this addiction, I will outlast this opposition. I have strength for all things." Out of those millions of people, the only ones that ever made it in to the Promised Land were Joshua and Caleb. It's not a coincidence that they were the only ones who thought power thoughts. You can't reach your destiny thinking negative, limiting thoughts. You have to think bold thoughts, favor thoughts, abundance thoughts, healing thoughts, victorious thoughts!

Faith Reflection

Is something stealing your joy today? Worries over a loved one, an unexpected bill, an issue with your health? I'm not saying ignore it. Doctors can do so much these days. I am saying to guard your heart and mind from negative thoughts. What's in front of you may be big, but our God is bigger. He is unchanging and is able to do abundantly more than you or I could ever ask or think (see Ephesians 3:20).

"Don't just think any thought that comes to mind. If it's negative, don't give it the time of day. God said He will never let you face anything that you can't handle. He will always give you the grace, the strength, the faith for what comes your way."

Joel

CHAPTER 3

RUNNING-OVER
Blessings

*"But seek first the kingdom of God and his righteousness,
and all these things will be added to you."*

Matthew 6:33, ESV

When you pour water into a glass, you stop when you come to the top. Of course. You are limited by the size of the container. But God says, "When I pour out a blessing, I'm not limited by your capacity to receive." You may have a small cup, small faith, small dreams. But if God only blessed us according to how much we believed, we would be limited. If it were just up to us, we would never see Ephesians 3:20, God doing ". . . exceedingly more than we can ask, or imagine."

But God is so good. He says, "Even when you have a little cup, even when you have small faith, that's not going to stop Me from the big blessing I have in store." He's not going to stop pouring at the top of your cup. He's going to give you a running-over blessing.

Keep God First Place

The Scripture says that when you honor God, blessings will chase you down (see Deuteronomy 28:2). You don't have to look for the blessings. Keep God first place, and the blessings will look for you. I believe right now promotion is looking for you, opportunity is looking for you, the right people, the healing, the business, the contract is looking for you. It's just a matter of time before you get the knock on the door, the phone call. You didn't see it coming; you couldn't have made it happen. What is that? It's the God of overflow doing more than you imagined, pouring out one of those blessings that you cannot contain.

This is what happened to Peter. In Luke 5, he had been fishing all night, doing his best, but he caught nothing. The next morning, he was on the shore cleaning his net when Jesus walked up and asked to borrow his boat. He had never met Peter, but Peter agreed. Jesus used the boat to teach the people from the shore. When He finished, He told Peter to go back out in the water, and put in his nets for a catch (see vv. 1–4).

Peter was a professional fisherman; he knew when to fish. This wasn't the right time. He said to Jesus, "We've worked all night and caught nothing; nevertheless, at Your word, we'll go back out" (v. 5, paraphrased). Peter threw his net out. Verse 6 says that they caught so many fish that their nets began to break. He had to call another boat over to come help him gather up all the fish. They had so many that both of their boats began to sink. They barely made it back to shore. Peter had caught fish many times, but he never had his nets break. He never had to call on others to help him.

We've all seen God's goodness in the past. We've seen Him open doors, we've seen Him turn things around; but you haven't seen anything yet. He has blessings coming for you — things you haven't seen, favor that you weren't prepared for, increase so amazing that you have to call for help, you can't handle it on your own.

Net-Breaking Blessings

I grew up watching the Houston Rockets play basketball at the Compaq Center. I had season tickets. But never in my wildest dreams did I think we would one day own the building! I just came to the games as a fan, like thousands of other people. But God's dream for your life is much bigger than your own. He has blessings that are going to catapult your family to a new level. When I became pastor and the church began to grow, I knew we needed a bigger place, but it never entered my mind to try to get the Compaq Center. It was so far outside of my thinking. Growing up, I had seen my father build sanctuary after sanctuary and add on to buildings. That was the normal way. That's what I was planning to do. "Let's find some land and build an auditorium," I thought.

But God is not always going to take you down a normal, traditional path. You're going to come into times where He's going to do something unprecedented — something that's never happened in your family, in your life. The "door" to the Compaq Center opened. God caused things to fall into place when the city council voted for us to have the building. I was astonished, amazed. I couldn't believe it happened. When I drive up now, I sometimes still get goosebumps. I recognize this is a net-breaking blessing.

GOD'S PROVISION *for You*

"... God's dream for your
life is much bigger than your
own. He has blessings that
are going to catapult your
family to a new level."

Joel

"Not Yet" Doesn't Mean "Never"

You may think, "Well Joel, I don't think this is for me. Last year wasn't too great. Business was slow. I've been at this same place a long time." May I tell you? You're right where Peter was. He had worked hard all night. He had done the right thing and caught nothing. He was tired, frustrated, thinking it was all a waste of time. Nothing looked like he was about to come in to overflow. It was just the opposite.

When it looks the worst, you don't see any sign of things changing. Thoughts tell you that you'll never get out of debt, never get well, never meet the right person. That's when you have to stay encouraged; you're on the verge of overflow. You are close to a net-breaking blessing. Jesus said to Peter, in effect, "Just because it didn't happen last night doesn't mean it's not going to happen in the morning." It may not have happened last year, but that doesn't mean it's not going to happen this year.

Maybe like Peter, you've done the right thing, you've worked hard, been faithful; but you caught nothing. Your time is coming. There weren't any fish out there last time, but God controls the fish. He knows how to bring the fish to you. It's not too late; you're not too old. Business may be down, or the medical report is not good. You're in prime position for overflow. God is saying, "Throw that net out one more time." Start believing again, start dreaming again, start taking steps of faith. You don't know what God is about to do. The reason it hasn't happened yet is because it's bigger than you think. It's not going to be a normal catch, an average contract, an ordinary promotion. It's going to be a net-breaking blessing — something unprecedented and favor so heavy that it starts to sink the boat.

Luke 5:9 says Peter was astonished at the amount of fish they caught. He was amazed, bewildered. He had never seen that kind of catch. God is going to do things in your life that astonish you. Doors will open that you never dreamed would open. He's going to put you in positions of influence and leadership that you never imagined. He's going to give you resources, funds, opportunity like you never dreamed. His idea of overflow is not just a little more of what you have; it's a new dimension. It's something unprecedented that you've never fathomed. It will astonish you!

"All these blessings
will come on you and
accompany you if you obey
the LORD your God: You will
be blessed in the city and
blessed in the country."

Deuteronomy 28:2–3, NIV

Faith Reflection

Amos 9:13 says the days are coming when everything barren and fruitless will overflow with blessings. This was written many years ago. I believe the day is not coming — the day is here. Whatever has been barren in your life, whatever area you've been lacking in, God is saying you're about to overflow with blessings, resources, good health, creativity, and overflow in your finances. I believe and declare you're about to be bursting at the seams. You're about to see favor that catapults you to a new level, increase that you cannot contain, in Jesus' name!

"When it looks the worst, when you don't see any sign of things changing, thoughts tell you that you'll never get out of debt, never get well, never meet the right person. That's when you have to stay encouraged. You're on the verge of overflow! You are close to a net-breaking blessing!"

Joel

CHAPTER 4

GOD IS YOUR
Gardener

"I am the true grapevine, and my Father is the gardener. He cuts off every branch of mine that doesn't produce fruit, and he prunes the branches that do bear fruit so they will produce even more."

John 15:1–2, NLT

We all go through times where we feel like we're going backwards. We were doing good, but then things turned, and we wonder what happened. What did we do wrong? Here's what I want you to see . . . just because you have difficulties and things you don't understand, it doesn't mean you're not in God's will.

Trusting God for Better

Just as there are seasons of growth, there are also seasons of pruning. Without the pruning, we wouldn't become all we were created to be. God won't let you go through a cutback if it's not going to eventually work for your good. It may be uncomfortable; you don't understand. You lost a contract, lost a relationship, lost an opportunity. God wouldn't have let you lose it if He weren't going to give you something better.

Jesus said in John 15:1–2, *"I am the true vine, and my Father is the gardener. He cuts off every branch in me that bears no fruit . . ."* (NIV). That makes sense. When we have things in our life that are not productive — a friend pulling us down, wasting time on the computer, or a job that's not leading anywhere — He'll cut those things away, so we can put our energy into things that are moving us forward. We can understand losing something that's not adding value to our lives. But He goes on to say in verse 2: *". . . every branch that bears fruit He prunes, that it may bear more fruit."* The only way to get from fruit to more fruit is to be cut back. There are times in life where you lose things that don't make sense. You're going to work with a good attitude, helping others, faithfully raising your children, doing the right thing, and then the wrong thing happens.

Instead of getting discouraged, slacking off, having no passion, recognize it's a pruning season. Without that cutback, you won't see new growth. You may be satisfied to stay where you are, not be uncomfortable, not rock the boat, but God is not satisfied. He loves you too much to let you miss your destiny. He has new levels in store for you, new opportunities, new relationships. Will you trust Him in the cutback seasons? Will you keep doing the right thing when you're in a time of pruning, when things have gone backwards, when you could be discouraged?

Jesus went on to say, verses 7–8, *"If you abide in Me . . . you [will] bear much fruit."* In this passage, He mentions fruit, more fruit, and much fruit. The way you move up, the way you increase is simply by abiding. He was saying, "When things happen that you don't understand, things that don't make sense, when you could be bitter, you could slack off, instead if you'll trust Me; keep doing the right thing, keep serving, keep giving, keep smiling, keep expecting favor, keep going the extra mile, and you'll pass the test. You'll come in to more fruit. When you prove to God that you'll be faithful in the cutback seasons, then He will release you into much fruit. He'll take you where you can't go on your own. But we won't see new levels without going through these seasons of losing things we don't understand, seasons that don't make sense, seasons where we're uncomfortable, seasons where what worked in the past is not working now. Don't get discouraged! That cutback season is all a part of the process. It's preparing you for new growth.

A Shift in Your Favor

I talked to a man whose company was sold, and they let all the employees go. He couldn't find a job for the longest time. He ended up having to move back home and live with his mother. He's in his fifties. He said, "I never dreamed I'd be here at my age. I don't know what happened." I told him what I'm telling you: you came into a cutback season. It's not a surprise to God. Whether you stay there or not depends on what you do. If you get bitter, complain, talk about how bad life is, go around defeated, then you'll get stuck. But when

"He loves you too much to let you miss your destiny. He has new levels in store for you, new opportunities, new relationships. Will you trust Him in the cutback seasons?"

Joel

you realize the cutback is a sign that new growth is coming, that more fruit is in your future, that God is getting you prepared for new levels, then things are going to change in your favor. You're going to see new doors begin to open. Let me encourage you: make the decision to thank Him, believe that He's in control, and go around being good to others.

I saw this man about six months later. He had a new job and had moved into a new house. He said, "I am happier and more fulfilled than I've ever been." Don't let the cutback fool you. The enemy didn't get control of the pruning shears. He didn't overtake God, and now he's ordering your steps. God is in control. You may not like the cutback. It may not make sense, but this is what faith is all about. "God, I don't understand it, but I trust you. I know you wouldn't have allowed this if You didn't have a purpose. I want to thank You that I'm not just going to come out; I'm going to come out better."

I wonder how many times we're fighting against things that God has ordained. I believe in standing against sickness, addictions, dysfunction; but every difficulty is not the enemy. It's the gardener. God prunes. He cuts us back, not to limit us but to prepare us for new growth. Are you discouraged over something you lost, something that hasn't worked out, thinking the enemy has hindered you, when in fact it's the hand of God? We give the enemy too much credit. He can't touch you without God's permission.

We believe God is directing our steps when good things are happening. It's easy to thank Him in the harvest seasons, the promotion seasons, the growing seasons, but when you come to a cutback season, you have to dig down deep. Your praise in the pruning seasons carries more weight than in the harvest seasons. You're not only showing God that you trust Him, but God is doing a work in you. Your character is being developed. Your spiritual muscles are getting stronger. We may not like the cutbacks but God is the gardener. He knows when something has to be cut back or we would get stuck. He knows not only when to prune, but He knows where to prune. He's not going to take something away that you needed. He's not going to cut something back without giving you more in return. Dare to trust Him.

Trust God's Purpose

A couple of years ago, I planted a row of trees along my fence in the backyard to help block the view. I bought the biggest ones I could find. They were about fifteen feet tall. They were the type that would form a thick hedge that you couldn't see through. They are outside my kitchen window, and I was constantly checking their growth, seeing how much they had filled in and how tall they were. I could measure how close they were getting to the telephone lines.

About six months later, the man that helps with my landscaping said that it was time to trim all the bushes and all the trees and asked if that was okay. I told him yes but to not touch the trees in the backyard because I wanted them to grow taller and help block the view. He said, "Okay but they won't grow like they should." I said, "What do you mean?" He said, "When we prune them it stimulates new growth. If we don't cut them back they won't fill out and get as tall as they could." I'm not a gardener. I thought just the opposite. "It's doing good, let it keep growing, don't bother it." But the

gardener knew if he didn't bother it, if he didn't take it through a cutback, it would actually limit its growth. Next year it wouldn't be what it should.

In the same way, God is your gardener. He's not going to cut you back if He doesn't have a purpose. He's not going to prune you if it's not going to lead to more fruit. It may not make sense to you; it may be uncomfortable. You feel like you're going the wrong direction, but you don't know what God is up to. The man said to me, "Let me trim them, and watch where they'll be next year. You'll be surprised at how full and tall they are." You may have been cutback, but God is saying, "Watch where you'll be next year. Watch which people are going to come into your life, watch what opportunities are going to come across your path, watch what doors are going to open." You're about to come in to a season of much fruit — a season where you see increase, promotion, friendships, good breaks like you've never seen.

Faith Reflection

Think of a time in your life when you experienced a disappointment, when what you hoped did not happen as you thought it would. With time, what can you now see about that situation that you couldn't see then? Maybe you have people in your life now you would have never met without going through that cutback. Perhaps you have a different job, live in a different place. Take a moment to give God thanks for His wisdom, favor, protection, and guidance.

"God is the gardener. He knows when something has to be cut back or we would get stuck. He knows not only when to prune, but He knows where to prune. He's not going to take something away that you needed. He's not going to cut something back without giving you more in return. Dare to trust Him."

Joel

CHAPTER 5

SOMETHING NEW
Is Coming

"See, I am doing a new thing! Now it springs up;
do you not perceive it? I am making a way in the
wilderness and streams in the wasteland."

Isaiah 43:19, NIV

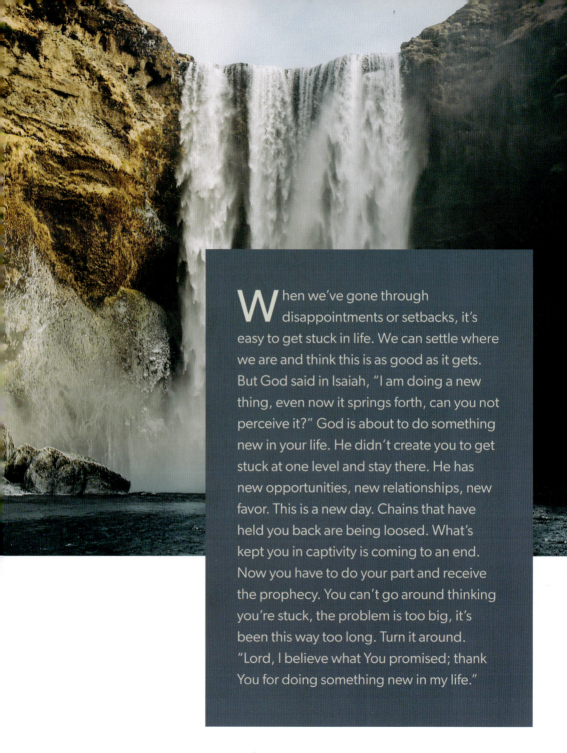

When we've gone through disappointments or setbacks, it's easy to get stuck in life. We can settle where we are and think this is as good as it gets. But God said in Isaiah, "I am doing a new thing, even now it springs forth, can you not perceive it?" God is about to do something new in your life. He didn't create you to get stuck at one level and stay there. He has new opportunities, new relationships, new favor. This is a new day. Chains that have held you back are being loosed. What's kept you in captivity is coming to an end. Now you have to do your part and receive the prophecy. You can't go around thinking you're stuck, the problem is too big, it's been this way too long. Turn it around. "Lord, I believe what You promised; thank You for doing something new in my life."

Receive the Prophecy

When Isaiah prophesied the new thing that God was doing, the Israelites were in captivity in Babylon. They had been there a long time, year after year, nothing changing. I'm sure they thought, "We'll always struggle; we'll always be oppressed." Then Isaiah showed up and said, "Get ready. God is doing a new thing." They could have thought, "Yeah right, have you seen these enemies? Look how powerful they are! All the circumstances say we're stuck, we'll never live an abundant life, we'll never own our own homes, our children will never be free." Don't talk yourself out of the new thing God wants to do. The odds may be against you, but the Most High God is for you.

The Israelites had been through many struggles, had unfair things happen. They made mistakes, brought the trouble on themselves. They could have been sitting in self-pity, discouraged. But Isaiah said, "Forget the former things, do not dwell on the past. Behold, God is doing a new thing." The principle is, if you're dwelling on the past, you won't see the new thing. God is saying, forget the former things, quit dwelling on your mistakes. This is a new day. Living in regrets will keep you from new opportunities; reliving your mistakes will stop the new favor. As long as you're looking back at the old, you won't see the new.

In your car, there's a big windshield in front of you and a very small rearview mirror. The reason it's so small is because what's behind you is not nearly as important as what's in front of you. Where you're going is what matters, not where you've been. Is there something you need to forget so you can see the new thing or something you need to quit dwelling on so you can step into the favor and abundance that God has for you?

When someone hurts you and you keep thinking about it, you're letting them continue to hurt you. Don't give them your power. You have to let it go. Give it to God. He saw what they did. He saw your tears, your heartache. He has beauty for those ashes. But here's the key: you have to let go of the ashes before you can see the beauty. It's an exchange. God says, "You give me the ashes, you quit dwelling on the hurts, you forgive them, you move forward with your life; and I'll give you the beauty. I'll do something so great, so rewarding that you don't even think about what you lost."

God Will Vindicate You

A lady told me how her relative had passed away and left her a small inheritance. She decided to invest it in real estate. She bought another house and was going to rent it out. The first people that came along seemed like fine people. They worked for a non-profit that helped children. She thought this couple would be perfect. She didn't do all the background checks that she should have. It turned out they were dishonest. Three months into the lease, they stopped paying rent and didn't tell her. She had it set up to go to the bank, and she thought everything was fine. They kept her from getting the notices. Several years went by, and eventually the house was foreclosed on; she lost all of her money. She could have been bitter, upset, tried to get revenge. But she said, "I didn't make a big deal about it." That takes maturity.

It's easy to make a big deal when we're hurt, betrayed. "Why did this happen? I'm going to get even." You have to forget the former things; do not dwell on the past. That means don't let the hurts, the bad breaks sour the rest of your life. God knows how to vindicate you. He knows how to pay you back.

"He saw your tears, your heartache. He has beauty for those ashes."

Joel

Six years later, this lady got a check in the mail unexpectedly from the bank, for $125,000. They said, "We sold the property, and this money belongs to you." She didn't even pay that much for it. She made a profit. God knows how to make rivers in the desert. He knows how to pay you back for the wrongs. This new thing He's going to do is going to be supernatural. He's going to turn barren ground into fertile ground. What looks like a loss is going to turn in to a gain. It seems like a setback, but really, it's a setup for God to show out in your life.

The desert represents barrenness, no growth. You're doing the right thing, but your business is not increasing, your marriage is not getting better, your health is not improving, you were passed over for another promotion. You're in the desert. In those dry places, you could be discouraged, thinking it will never change. No, get ready. God is about to make rivers in that desert. He's about to turn that barren land into fertile ground. Like that lady, you're going to see increase that you can't explain, favor that you didn't deserve, healing that doesn't make sense, freedom from things that have held you back.

Receive God's Blessings

When Isaiah prophesied this, the people could have said, "Thanks, Isaiah, but we've had too many bad breaks; this opposition is too big; we'll never get out." You can stop the prophecy from coming to pass. The psalmist said, "They limited the Holy One of Israel." You can limit what God wants to do in your life by doubt, negativity, speaking defeat. "My business is never going to grow. I'll never meet the right person. I haven't had a date in years. Have you seen all that I've been through?" You are canceling out the prophecy. You may have obstacles that look too big, you don't see how you can accomplish that dream. It feels like you're stuck, you're in captivity, restricted by your environment. God is saying to you what He said to them: "I am doing a new thing. I'm making rivers in those deserts. I'm turning the barren places into fertile ground." Now get in agreement with God. "Yes, Lord this is for me today. I receive it into my spirit. I'm getting ready for something new. Lord, amaze me with Your goodness. Turn this problem around. God, show out in my life."

You may not see how. That's okay. It's not up to you. It's up to God. He's the one that makes rivers in the desert. He's the one that parts seas, cures the lepers, multiplies food to feed thousands. The new thing God has for you, the new people, the new opportunities, the promotion, healing, and influence will be better than you ever dreamed!

"See, I am doing a new thing! Now it springs up; do you not perceive it? I am making a way in the wilderness and streams in the wasteland."

Isaiah 43:19, NIV

Faith Reflection

What "ashes" do you need to give to God today? He has beauty, blessing, goodness, healing. But you have to exchange what's holding you back to see the new thing He is doing. Take as long as you need, maybe a few minutes, maybe days, weeks, months. Pray, journal, talk with a trusted person in your life. Know that God loves you and longs to show you that infinite love in ways that you will know; the new things headed your way could have only come from Him.

"In your car, there's a big windshield in front of you and a very small rearview mirror. The reason it's so small is because what's behind you is not nearly as important as what's in front of you. Where you're going is what matters, not where you've been. Is there something you need to forget so you can see the new thing, something you need to quit dwelling on so you can step into the favor and abundance that God has for you?"

Joel

CHAPTER 6

GOING THE
Extra Mile

*"Trust in the LORD with all your heart, and do not lean on
your own understanding. In all your ways acknowledge
him, and he will make straight your paths."*

Proverbs 3:5–6, ESV

There are times in life when God asks us to do things that are hard, things that don't make sense — to give something to others when we need it more than them, to take a step of faith when we don't have the experience, to forgive someone that doesn't deserve it. Everything in our logic says, "This is not right; that's too much." In these times, God is asking you to go the extra mile. Anytime you obey, there's a blessing that follows. When you do the hard thing that God is asking you to do, it's not because He is trying to make your life miserable. It's because He has something awesome coming your way. He's setting you up for promotion, divine connections, favor that you've never seen. You can't reach the fullness of your destiny without extra-mile obedience.

Extra-Mile Obedience

In **1 Kings 17**, there was a widow who lived in the city of Zarephath. Her husband had died, and now she lived with her one son. There was a drought in the land that had dried up all the crops. She couldn't find any food. All she had left was a little flour and a little oil — just enough for one meal. She was out picking up sticks to build a fire. She was going to cook her last meal. She had already accepted, once they ate it, this was it.

A few days earlier the prophet Elijah was at the Jordan River, where he had been living. Every morning, the ravens would come to him. That's how he survived. Then the ravens quit coming. God said to him in verse 8, *"Go at once to Zarephath in the region of Sidon and stay there. I have directed a widow there to supply you with food"* (NIV). It's interesting that God sent him to a widow that didn't have any food. When God does things that don't make sense, that means He's up to something out of the ordinary — something supernatural is about to happen.

Elijah walked into town and saw the widow gathering the firewood. He said in verse 10, *"Would you bring me a little water . . . so I may have a drink?"* That was no problem. She was kind, she was giving, she stopped what she was doing, despite her own challenges, and went to get the water. Most of us are like her, if it's not too much, we're going to do it. if it's a small thing, no problem. But here's the test: as she was going to get the water, Elijah said in verse 11, *"As she was going to get it, he called, 'And bring me, please, a piece of bread.'"* The water was easy, but the meal was hard. Verse 12: *"'As surely as the LORD your God lives,' she replied, 'I don't have any bread—only a handful of flour in a jar and a little olive oil in a jug. I am gathering a few sticks to take home and make a meal for myself and my son, that we may eat it—and die.'"*

You would think Elijah would say, "I'm sorry, ma'am, I'm going to try to help you. I'm going to find you some food." Instead, after she had just poured out her heart, after she just swore that she didn't have any extra food, Elijah said, in verses 13 and 14, *"Don't be afraid. Go home and do as you have said. But first make a small loaf of bread for me from what you have and bring it to me, and then make something for yourself and your son. For this is what the LORD, the God of Israel, says: 'The jar of flour will not be used up and the jug of oil will not run dry until the day the LORD sends rain on the land.'"*

Elijah was saying, if you'll have extra-mile obedience, if you'll do something that doesn't make sense or that doesn't seem logical, you'll see an extra-mile blessing; you'll see supernatural provision, supernatural increase.

The Greater Your Blessing

The widow didn't understand. Her thoughts told her, "You're making a mistake. This couldn't be God; my son and I should be eating this meal." But this woman dared to obey. She took that step of faith and made him a meal first.

Verse 16 says, *"For the jar of flour was not used up and the jug of oil did not run dry, in keeping with the word of the LORD spoken by Elijah."* When you have extra-mile obedience, you set miracles into motion. God begins to pour out blessings, open up doors, bring supernatural provision, supernatural healing — things that you couldn't make happen, that will thrust you into new levels of your destiny. Are you

". . . if you'll do something that doesn't make sense or that doesn't seem logical, you'll see an extra-mile blessing; you'll see supernatural provision, supernatural increase."

Joel

missing the great things God wants to do because you're not willing to do the hard things? Don't talk yourself out of it. The more difficult it is, the greater the blessing.

God could have had Elijah show up and tell the woman, "God wants you to know that He sees you're struggling, and He's going to supply all your needs." He could have done it without her feeding Elijah, but most of the time, an act of obedience is required. If you'll do the hard thing when it doesn't seem logical or you don't feel like it and everything in your intellect is telling you this doesn't make sense, if you'll have this extra-mile obedience, you'll see God show out in your life.

He wouldn't ask you to do something hard unless He had something amazing coming. Is He asking you to forgive someone that hurt you? You've been holding on to the hurt for years. They don't deserve it; they were wrong. You're not excusing their behavior. You're letting go of the poison. If you could see what God has in store for you on the other side of that forgiveness, you wouldn't think twice. There are extra-mile blessings, new relationships, new opportunities, greater joy.

Set Your Miracle in Motion

Think about Joseph: his brothers betrayed him. He went through thirteen years of injustice, rejection, being in prison, and his dreams shattered all because of his brothers' jealousy. One day they showed up at the palace; now he was in charge, vindicated, promoted. His brothers were standing before him trying to buy food in a famine. This was Joseph's big chance to pay them back, get even, and everything in him said, "Treat them like they treated you." But

Joseph heard the still small voice saying, "Forgive; be good to them. Let it go."

It's one thing to forgive when someone is rude to you at the office — that doesn't take a lot of effort; but these brothers sold Joseph into slavery, they took his freedom, he lost years of his life being away from his family, not following his dream because of what they did to him. He had a right to be angry, get revenge, but Joseph understood this principle. He had extra-mile obedience. He forgave people that didn't deserve it. He forgave people that tried to ruin his life. Because God could trust him to do the hard thing, to forgive when it wasn't fair, to be good to people that weren't good to him, God poured out extra-mile blessings. He put Joseph in charge of the whole nation. When you have extra-mile obedience, you do what God's asking you to do when it's hard, when it's not fair, or when it doesn't make sense; there's no limit to how high God will take you.

Is God asking you to break away from people who are pulling you down? You know they're a negative influence, causing you to compromise. "But Joel, they've been my friends for years. We always hang out." I know it's not easy but where could you go, what could you become, if you did the hard thing? God wouldn't be asking you if He didn't have extra-mile blessings in store.

Is God asking you to keep a good attitude in a negative situation? You're working hard but not seeing growth; praying for your child but they're not changing; you lost a client, business has slowed. You're tempted to be critical, complain, live sour. Do the hard thing. Keep being your best, keep thanking God, keep being good to people, and keep declaring the victory.

When you do the hard thing, you set miracles into motion, angels go to work, good breaks come looking for you. There are good breaks, increase, and healing that are only connected to doing the right thing when it's hard. When you pass the test, you will come in to moments that thrust you into your God-given purpose!

Faith Reflection

What God asks you to do is not always going to make sense. Reflect on a situation in your life where you sense God's still, small voice. Maybe you're being asked to forgive someone you said you would never forgive. Maybe He is calling you to follow your heart in a certain area, but it is beyond your comfort zone. It's not always going to be logical. That's what faith is all about.

"If you'll do the hard thing
when it doesn't seem logical,
when you don't feel like it and
everything in your intellect is
telling you this doesn't make
sense, if you'll have this extra
mile obedience, you'll see
God show out in your life.
He wouldn't ask you to do
something hard unless He had
something amazing coming!"

Joel

CHAPTER 7

FROM CEASING TO
Increasing

*"And my God will supply every need of yours
according to his riches in glory in Christ Jesus."*

Philippians 4:19, ESV

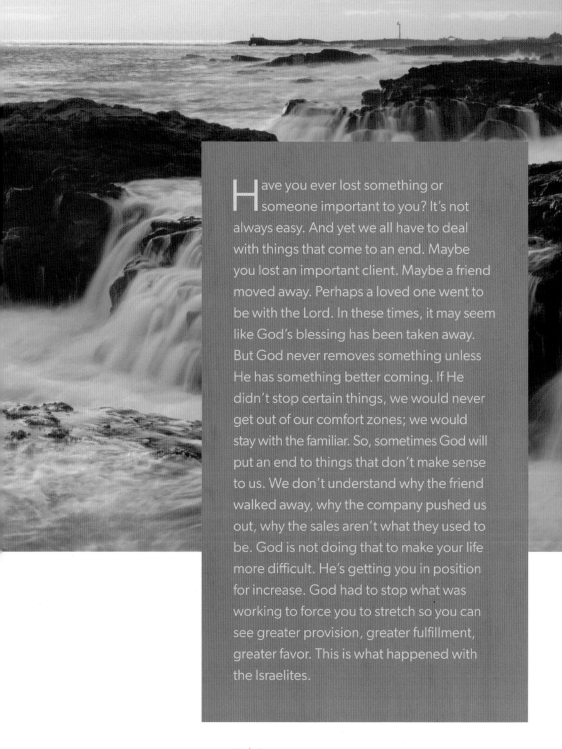

Have you ever lost something or someone important to you? It's not always easy. And yet we all have to deal with things that come to an end. Maybe you lost an important client. Maybe a friend moved away. Perhaps a loved one went to be with the Lord. In these times, it may seem like God's blessing has been taken away. But God never removes something unless He has something better coming. If He didn't stop certain things, we would never get out of our comfort zones; we would stay with the familiar. So, sometimes God will put an end to things that don't make sense to us. We don't understand why the friend walked away, why the company pushed us out, why the sales aren't what they used to be. God is not doing that to make your life more difficult. He's getting you in position for increase. God had to stop what was working to force you to stretch so you can see greater provision, greater fulfillment, greater favor. This is what happened with the Israelites.

God's Purpose for Manna

The Israelites had been in slavery for many years when God supernaturally brought them out. But they had a big problem. They didn't have anything to eat. There was no way to survive out there in the desert. But every morning, God gave them something called manna. It was like bread that formed on the ground. For forty years, one thing they could always count on was the manna. They had enemies to fight. They had to overcome the heat. There were snakes and scorpions, but every morning, like clockwork, there was the manna. They knew that was the hand of God taking care of them. What they didn't realize was, the manna was only temporary provision. They became satisfied. But God wasn't satisfied. He was taking them into a land flowing with milk and honey — a land filled with all kinds of fruits, vegetables, and resources.

Then, something interesting happened when they got close to the Promised Land. The Scripture says, in Joshua 5:12 that the manna ceased, and they never saw the manna again. I can hear them panicking, "God, what's happening? You've brought us this far, why are you leaving us now? Why won't you provide anymore?" They would have lived off the manna the rest of their lives. So, God, on purpose, stopped the manna. He basically said to them, "From now on, I want you to cook your own food. There's provision all around you. You don't need this manna to sustain you. I'm bringing you into abundance." It wasn't a coincidence that the manna stopped when they were about to enter into the Promised Land. When something ceases in your life, it's an indication that increase is coming. God doesn't stop things unless He has greater provision on the way.

What you were satisfied with was only temporary provision. You were blessed, life was good; but God has so much more. He had to cease that friendship. He had to move that person out of your life, not because they're not good, but because they're limiting you. They can't go where you're going. God had to shut that door so He can bring people into your life who will push you into your destiny — people who will help you, not hinder you.

When the manna quits appearing, instead of being discouraged, have a new perspective: you're on the verge of a new level. That's a sign that you're about to take new ground. Walls are about to come down. Giants are about to be defeated. You're going to step into favor, increase, healing, and breakthroughs like you've never seen.

Winning Big

My friend Tony Dungy played professional football for many years. After a great career, in 1996, he landed his first job as a head coach with the Tampa Bay Buccaneers. He didn't know anyone there. He didn't have any special contacts, but out of a half dozen other very experienced, qualified candidates, he was chosen. He knew it was the hand of God opening that door — a dream come true. For six years, everything went great. They were winning more games, making more progress. The manna — the provision, the favor — was there each morning. But one day, unexpectedly, he was let go. They fired him. He thought, "God, I know you opened this door. I know Your favor put me here. I don't understand what happened." God never ceases something without having something better on the way.

"When something ceases
in your life, it's an indication
that increase is coming.
God doesn't stop things
unless He has greater
provision on the way."

Joel

You have to understand: the reason the manna stops, the reason doors close, the reason people walk away is because you're close to your promised land. That's God taking away the temporary provision. The manna may look permanent to us. We're satisfied. But God's dream for your life is much bigger than our own.

Coach Dungy was disappointed, but he didn't sit around discouraged in self-pity, thinking about what didn't work out. He started thanking God that something else was going to open up. He knew the same God that opened the door in Tampa Bay had closed that door. The same God that directed his steps to that position had directed his steps away from that position. Not long after he was let go, he received a phone call from the Indianapolis Colts. They said, "We're looking for a new coach. Would you be interested?" Coach Dungy took the job. He went on to win the Super Bowl with the Colts. What looked like a great disappointment, the manna ceasing, getting pushed out, was really a great blessing!

Entering into Abundance

As for the Israelites, the closer they got to the Promised Land, the less God did for them. The closer they got, the more they had to grow up. God expected them to stand on their own two feet, to encourage themselves, to fight off fear. He was saying, "The day is over when I'm going to bring you the manna. You have provision all around you. I brought you this far, I've fought all the battles, I've given you breakfast every morning but for this next level, to enter into this place of abundance. You're going to have to do your part."

The Israelites had to accept that having no manna meant it was a new day, and God was doing a new thing. If they had been sour about the manna ceasing, they wouldn't have seen the walls of Jericho come down; they wouldn't have conquered city after city and lived in the land of abundance.

With the Promised Land comes new levels of responsibility. Maybe in the past you've relied on others to encourage you and keep you cheered up. God's going to wean those people away — not because God doesn't love you, but because He wants you to stand on your own. You can't reach your destiny always depending on someone else. You don't need that crutch. Start encouraging yourself. All through the day, say in your mind, "I am strong in the LORD; something good is going to happen to me. God being for me is more than the world being against me."

God has something much bigger, much better in mind. Maybe the manna has ceased in some area of your life. You are tempted to give up on a dream, to lose your passion. But that ending in your life means that greater provision is coming. It is God repositioning you to do something you've never seen. This is not the time to get discouraged. It's time to get ready and stir your faith up! You are close to your promised land!

"Then the manna ceased on the day after they had eaten the produce of the land; and the children of Israel no longer had manna, but they ate the food of the land of Canaan that year."

Joshua 5:12, NKJV

Faith Reflection

Are you letting what's ceased in your life cause you to be sour, discouraged, or are you seeing it as a sign that you're about to go into your promised land? When things cease, you have to dig your heels in, "This business may have slowed down, but God, I know You're about to open new doors. This person walked away, but God, I thank You that you have someone better coming. This marriage is more difficult, but Lord, I thank You that joy, peace, favor are on the way."

"God never ceases something without having something better on the way!"

Joel

CHAPTER 8

YOUR ANOINTING IS
Unique

*"He who has prepared us for this very thing is God,
who has given us the Spirit as a guarantee."*

2 Corinthians 5:5, ESV

What God has prepared for you is not affected by people or circumstances. His blessing will catapult you beyond what people thought and put you into the fullness of your destiny.

Impossible . . . in the Natural

I have a friend who was planning to build a new sanctuary. It was going to cost about $40 million. He was raising the funds and starting to draw up the plans. One day out of the blue, the mayor called him and told how there was a group that built a huge building for a casino, but before they moved in, they went bankrupt. They had over forty acres of parking, a building that could fit four football fields inside, and it was just a few miles from his church. The mayor asked if he was interested in purchasing it. The pastor thought it would be at least $50 million; it was huge ... first class. The mayor said, "No, you can purchase it for under $2 million." A man that owned a production company got word that the pastor was interested. He said, "I've got a big screen that's used for concerts and sporting events. It's over a hundred and fifty feet long. It cost $3 million new, but I'll sell it to you for $50,000." Things began to fall into place. Instead of my friend having to build a new facility, God dropped a much bigger and better facility into their hands. That was a blessing stored up — something that God had already prepared; and at the right time, God released it.

If you could see what God has stored up for you — the blessings He has prepared, the people you're going to meet, the places you're going to go, the good breaks that are going to find you — it would boggle your mind. You're going to see the surpassing greatness of God's favor.

Too often we look at our circumstances and come up with excuses as to why it's not going to happen: "Joel, I don't have the training, the talent, the connections; I'm the wrong nationality, I'm too short.

I'll never come into my blessing." No, God is not limited by our circumstances, by what family we come from, by who's against us. When God breathed His life into you, He placed a blessing on you that overrides anything that's trying to hold you back. The blessing God has for you cannot be stopped by bad breaks, by people, by injustice. God has the final say. The garden He has prepared for you, He has every intention of bringing you into it.

Your Overriding Blessing

In the Scripture, we see David as a powerful king, a great man — one of the heroes of faith. But it's interesting that David didn't come from a royal family. He hadn't been trained to take the throne. He wasn't raised in wealth or influence. His family was very poor. He was the eighth son of a man named Jesse. His brothers were all involved in the army and had prestigious positions, but David's job was to take care of his father's sheep. He was looked down on, seen as secondary. His family thought, "He'll never amount to much. Let's just stick him out in the shepherd's field." It didn't look like he had much of a future: a low-income family, no education, and his own father didn't believe in him.

But just because people write you off doesn't mean God writes you off. Circumstances may look like, "You're stuck, too bad, you'll never get out of this." But that doesn't change what God has prepared for you. The blessing God put on you will override any curse. The blessing will make up for what you didn't get. The blessing will make up for people not being for you. The blessing will make up for any disadvantage.

"If you could see what God has stored up for you — the blessings He has prepared, the people you're going to meet, the places you're going to go, the good breaks that are going to find you — it would boggle your mind."

Joel

The prophet Samuel visited Jesse's house to anoint one of Jesse's sons as the next king of Israel. Seven of his sons were in the house, all lined up. Jesse was so proud. Samuel went down the row, one by one. He turned the bottle over to pour the oil out and anoint the first son, but the oil wouldn't flow. He thought, "It's not this one." He moved to the second son. He tried to pour it, but the oil wouldn't flow. Samuel moved to the next one, the same thing, the next and next. He went through all seven sons, but the oil never flowed. Samuel was confused. He knew God had spoken to him that it would be a son of Jesse. He said to Jesse, "Something's wrong. It's not any of these sons. I must have missed it." Jesse said, "Well, I do have one other son. His name is David, but I'm sure it's not him. He's the youngest. He's small. He'll never amount to much." Samuel said, "Bring him in." David stood before him, and Samuel poured the oil. It began to flow and flow. He knew right then that David was the next king.

Here's the point: you don't have to worry about somebody else getting your blessing. The oil that's prepared for you will not flow to anyone else. When Samuel tried to anoint the other sons, the oil defied gravity. I can see Samuel turning the bottle over, hitting the top, but the oil would not come until it recognized the right person that was supposed to be blessed.

When it's your time to be blessed, don't worry; nobody can take your blessing. The blessing that's prepared for you will not flow out to anyone else. You may think, "My coworker got the promotion that I deserved; I worked so hard, but my supervisor overlooked me." No, if you didn't get it, it wasn't supposed to be yours. Like with David, your oil is not going to flow for somebody else. The blessing that belongs to you will be your blessing. Nobody can take it.

Follow God's Lead

In the Scripture, Elijah was living in a certain city, when God said to him, **"Leave here, turn eastward and hide in the Kerith Ravine, east of the Jordan. You will drink from the brook, and I have directed the ravens to supply you with food there." (1 Kings 17:3–4, NIV)** When he got to that brook every day, just like clockwork, the ravens would come. Elijah had his provision, a prepared blessing. Here's the key: he didn't have to find the ravens. He just had to get where God wanted him to be, and the ravens found him.

In the same way, there is a place where God has commanded you to be blessed. The ravens are already there, your provision, your favor, your increase. The prepared blessing is waiting on you. The question is, will you do what's required? Elijah could have said, "God I don't want to leave this place, I like it here. I'm comfortable, my friends are here." The problem is if he would have stayed, he would have missed where He was commanded to be blessed. He could have survived, he could have endured; but if you want to see God's best, you've got to be willing to do what you know God's asking you to do.

Maybe deep down, you know you're supposed to get away from some friends that are a bad influence. They're dragging you down, causing you to be negative, to compromise. As long as you stay there, you're going to miss your prepared blessing. God has something more — more favor, more increase, more provision.

But you've got to be willing to make the changes. "Well, Joel, if I do that, I'll be lonely. I won't have any friends." Yes, you may be lonely for a season, but God will always bring you new friends. He'll bring you better friends. It may be difficult for a time, but before long, you'll come into that prepared blessing. The ravens will be there — greater joy, greater fulfilment, new relationships. It may not be leaving friends or moving physically. It may just be in your mind. You need to leave the negative thoughts, leave the worry, leave the anxiety, leave the offense, the resentment, the anger. God has a place of abundance for you, a place where He's commanded you to be blessed, but you've got to do your part and leave what He's asking you to leave. It may mean you have to get out of your comfort zone and take a step of faith. You can't play it safe all your life and expect to reach your highest potential.

Faith Reflection

You need to get ready. God's about to bring you into something that He's already finished. It has your name on it. It's going to be bigger, better, more rewarding than you ever imagined. Stay in faith, keep doing what God asks you do to, leave what He asks you to leave. If you'll do this, I believe and declare you are going to come in to prepared blessings, favor that you didn't earn, good breaks that you didn't deserve, increase, promotion, the fullness of your destiny, in Jesus' name.

"You can't play it safe all your life and expect to reach your highest potential. It may mean you have to get out of your comfort zone and take a step of faith."

Joel

CHAPTER 9

THE POWER OF YOUR
Thoughts

". . . Let the weak say, 'I am strong.' "

Joel 3:10, NKJV

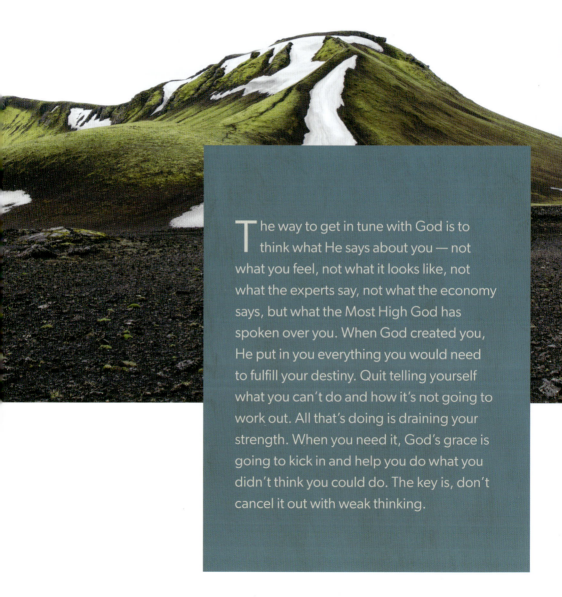

The way to get in tune with God is to think what He says about you — not what you feel, not what it looks like, not what the experts say, not what the economy says, but what the Most High God has spoken over you. When God created you, He put in you everything you would need to fulfill your destiny. Quit telling yourself what you can't do and how it's not going to work out. All that's doing is draining your strength. When you need it, God's grace is going to kick in and help you do what you didn't think you could do. The key is, don't cancel it out with weak thinking.

Right Thinking Changes Things

When my father went to be with the Lord and I stepped up to pastor the church, every thought told me that I couldn't do it. I wasn't qualified. I didn't have the training. I was too quiet. But if I would have believed that report, you wouldn't be reading this, and I would have missed my destiny. The Scripture says, *"Be careful what you think."* (Proverbs 4:23, NCV) It gives us a warning. Your thoughts are setting the limits for your life. During that time, all that came to my mind were negative, fearful, intimidating thoughts. But here's the thing: I didn't dwell on them and think they were the truth. I tuned them out and got in tune with God. On purpose, I thought, "I can do all things through Christ; I am strong in the Lord. I've been raised up for such a time as this. Father, thank You that I'm equipped, empowered, and anointed."

When my thoughts would tell me, "Nobody's going to listen to you, Joel. You don't have anything to say." Instead of believing those lies, I would say, "Father, thank You that Your favor is causing me to stand out. Thank You that people are going to like me; they're going to be drawn to me." If I hadn't gotten in tune with God and thought these power thoughts, I wouldn't be here.

Power Up Every Day

Your thoughts may tell you, "You've been through too much. You lost a loved one, the business didn't make it, that friend walked out on you. Nothing good is in your future." Don't believe those lies. Declare with me right now, "Father, thank You that You have beauty for ashes. Thank You that what was meant for my harm, You're turning to my advantage." When you're in tune with God, He'll pay you back for the wrongs. Isaiah said that He will give you double for the unfair things that happened (see Isaiah 61:7). Instead of thinking you've seen your best days, think this: "Lord, thank You that double is coming. Thank You that my latter days will be better than my former days."

Psalm 125:4 says *"O LORD, do good to those who are good, whose hearts are in tune with you"* (NLT). Notice that you can be in tune or out of tune with God. The way you get in tune is by thinking victorious, overcoming, faith-filled thoughts. If you go around thinking, "I'll never get well. This depression, this anxiety, this addiction is going to hinder me all of my life," then unfortunately you're not in tune with God. You can't find anywhere in the Scripture where God says, "I'm weak, I'm discouraged, I'm afraid, the enemy is getting the best of me." God says, "I am all powerful. I spoke worlds into existence. I flung stars into space." Moses asked God what His name was. He said, "Moses, My name is I Am." He was saying, "I am everything. I am strength, I am healing, I am provision, I am abundance, I am protection, I am favor. When God said, *"Let there be light,"* (Genesis 1:3, NLT), it came at 186,000 miles per second. One angel in the Old Testament destroyed 185,000 of the enemies of Israel (see 2 Kings 19:35). If you're going to get in tune with Him, you can't think little, weak, defeated, get-by, hope-this-works-out thoughts.

Every morning when you wake up, you need to power up. Get your mind going in the right direction. "This is going to be a good day. I can handle anything that comes my way. I am strong, I am confident. I have the favor of God. Angels are watching over me. I'm excited about my future." At the start of the day, you need to set your mind for victory. Don't let just any thoughts play. You have to think thoughts on purpose. If you wake up and just think whatever

"Every morning when you wake up, you need to power up. Get your mind going in the right direction."

Joel

comes to mind, thoughts will tell you, "You have too many problems, you're too tired, you'll never overcome this obstacle. Nothing good is going to happen today." If you don't set the tone for the day, negative thoughts will set them for you. Before you check your phone, before you read your email, before you see what the weather is like, you need to think power thoughts, victory thoughts, abundance thoughts, can-do thoughts on purpose.

You Are Destined to Reign

In the Scripture, there was a young man named Mephibosheth. He was the grandson of King Saul, and the son of Jonathan, David's best friend. Mephibosheth was born into royalty, destined to one day take the throne. But when he was five years old, his grandfather and father were killed in the battle. When word reached his house, the maid that took care of him picked him up and took off running, afraid that the enemy army was going to come after them. In her haste, she accidentally tripped and dropped Mephibosheth. Both of his legs were broken. He became crippled for life. Sometimes, well-meaning people can drop you. This nurse had good intentions; she was trying to help him, but she dropped him. Years passed, and Mephibosheth ended up living exiled in a city called Lodebar. It was one of the poorest, most rundown cities of that day. The name Lodebar means "without pasture." It had no greenery, no place to grow crops. It was like a wasteland. Here, Mephibosheth was the grandson of a king; he had royalty in his blood, but now he was in the slums, barely surviving.

One day, King David was thinking about his friend Jonathan. He asked his men if there were any of his relatives still alive so he could be good to them. David's men went out and searched through the slums of Lodebar and finally found Mephibosheth. Now he was a grown man. They had to carry him back to the palace. I'm sure Mephibosheth was afraid, thinking David was going to pay him back for his grandfather, King Saul trying to kill him. But it was just the opposite. David was incredibly kind to him. He said, "From now on, you're going to live in the palace with me. Every night, you're going to have dinner at my table. I'm going to give you all the land that belonged to your grandfather, King Saul. Mephibosheth was overwhelmed. He couldn't believe what was happening. But the way he answered shows us why he was living in Lodebar all those years. He said to David, **2 Samuel 9:8, "Who is your servant, that you should show such kindness to a dead dog like me?"** Notice how his thoughts were weak, defeated: "I don't deserve to be blessed. I've had too many bad breaks; people dropped me."

I wonder how many of us are acting like Mephibosheth. We are sons and daughters of the Most High God. We have royalty in our blood; we're destined to reign in life. But because we've been dropped, somebody did us wrong, we went through disappointments, things that weren't fair . . . Or, we made mistakes, we got off course, brought trouble on ourselves and now we're living in Lodebar, thinking we don't deserve to be blessed. We just have to sit on the sidelines, make it through life, accept that our dreams will never come to pass. Can I encourage you? Get rid of that dead-dog thinking. Nothing that's happened to you has to keep you from your destiny. You may have had some bad breaks but that didn't stop God's plan for your life. Now you have to do your part: quit thinking limited, defeated, unworthy thoughts and start thinking victory thoughts, abundance thoughts, favor thoughts.

Put your shoulders back, hold your head up high, and remember who you are and whose you are — a child of the Most High God. Get in tune with Him. Like David's men went searching through Lodebar, God is looking for you today. He's saying, "I'm about a do a new thing. I'm about to pay you back for the wrongs. I'm about to open new doors, turn negative situations around. Like Mephibosheth, you're going to be amazed at the goodness of God."

I'm asking you to pay attention to what you're thinking about. You are drawing in what you're constantly dwelling on. Your thoughts are running your life. Is what you're thinking about what you want? Are you thinking weak, defeated, I-can't-do-it thoughts, or are you thinking power thoughts: "I am well able, God is fighting my battles, something good is in my future." Don't be like the ten spies, the eighty percent that are negative; stand out in the crowd. Be a Joshua, be a Caleb and think victory thoughts. If you'll do this, I believe and declare, like God did for them, you're going to make it into your promised land. You're going to see God show out in your life. Like Mephibosheth, everything you've lost, God is about to restore. The health, the finances, the dreams — they're going to come looking for you, in Jesus' name.

Faith Reflection

Is there an area in your life where negative thoughts are telling you, "You're just average, there's nothing special about you"? Now is the time to get rid of those defeated thoughts and replace them with power thoughts — with what God says about you: "You are fearfully and wonderfully made. You are a masterpiece. You have royal blood flowing through your veins. You are crowned with favor. You will leave your mark." If you'll get in tune with God, He'll open doors no person can shut. He'll take you where you can't go on your own!

"You may have had some bad breaks, but that didn't stop God's plan for your life. Now you have to do your part: quit thinking limited, defeated, unworthy thoughts and start thinking victory thoughts, abundance thoughts, favor thoughts!"

Joel

CHAPTER 10

DIFFICULTY CAN'T STOP
God's Blessing

*"You crown the year with a bountiful harvest;
even the hard pathways overflow with abundance."*

Psalm 65:11, NLT

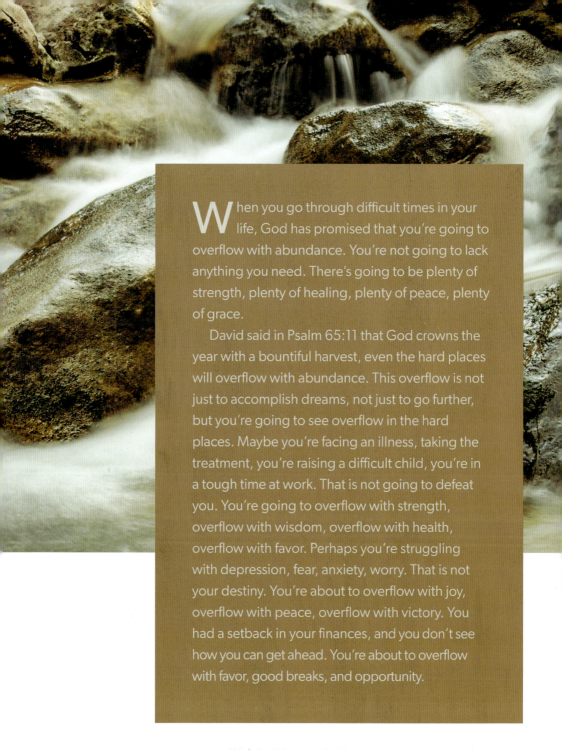

When you go through difficult times in your life, God has promised that you're going to overflow with abundance. You're not going to lack anything you need. There's going to be plenty of strength, plenty of healing, plenty of peace, plenty of grace.

David said in Psalm 65:11 that God crowns the year with a bountiful harvest, even the hard places will overflow with abundance. This overflow is not just to accomplish dreams, not just to go further, but you're going to see overflow in the hard places. Maybe you're facing an illness, taking the treatment, you're raising a difficult child, you're in a tough time at work. That is not going to defeat you. You're going to overflow with strength, overflow with wisdom, overflow with health, overflow with favor. Perhaps you're struggling with depression, fear, anxiety, worry. That is not your destiny. You're about to overflow with joy, overflow with peace, overflow with victory. You had a setback in your finances, and you don't see how you can get ahead. You're about to overflow with favor, good breaks, and opportunity.

Blessed to Bless Others

God didn't create us to just get by in life or to just have enough for what we need. We're grateful for that, but God is not a get-by God: He's an overflow God. He wants you to have an abundance so you can be a blessing to others. Where you have so much joy, you bring joy wherever you go. You have so many resources, you can help those around you. You may not have seen this yet, but God is about to do a new thing. He has explosive blessings — blessings that catapult you to a new level. One touch of His favor will take you from having just enough to having more than enough. You need to get ready; overflow is coming. You're going to overflow with creativity, with talent, with ideas. Overflow with good relationships, with great people in your life. Overflow with influence, with respect, with promotion. Overflow with opportunity, with resources, where you come out of debt, where you lend and not borrow. Get in agreement with God. "Lord, thank You that overflow is coming. Thank You that You're a more-than-enough God."

In the Scripture, Jesus was out in the desert teaching the people. It was late in the day, and they were all hungry. He told the disciples to feed them. They were out in the middle of nowhere. They said, "Jesus, all we have is five loaves of bread and two fish." Jesus told his disciples to have them sit in groups of fifty and a hundred. They went out and counted the people and put them in these groups. There were five thousand men there, plus the women and children. Jesus prayed over the food, and it multiplied. As they served the people, the food kept coming. When it was all over, they had twelve baskets full of food left over.

What's interesting is, Jesus knew exactly how many people were there. He had the disciples take time to count. He could have had the food stop multiplying when everyone was fed. After all, God is precise; He is detailed. He doesn't make mistakes. It's not like He miscalculated or accidentally made too much food. On purpose, God designed there would be overflow. He was showing us His nature. He not only supplies our needs, but He's an overflow God — a God of more than enough.

Your Destiny Is Abundance

When God laid out the plan for your life, He calculated exactly what you would need. He knows what it's going to take to get you to your destiny; then on purpose, He put in extra. When your needs were met, He said in effect, "Let me keep multiplying; let me give them more than enough." He's already designed the overflow for you. He's already set up the good breaks, the promotion, the right people, the healing, the favor. You're going to come into these times where God shows out in your life. You didn't have the experience, you weren't next in line; but suddenly you're promoted, suddenly you meet the right person, suddenly you're out of debt. You weren't looking for it; the blessing came looking for you.

Sometimes people will try to convince you that you're not supposed to be blessed. In seminary, my father was taught that he was supposed to be poor to show that he was humble. One of the names of God is El Shaddai. That means "more than enough." If God just wanted you to get by, if He just wanted you to have enough, why would His name be "more than enough"? Don't let people talk you out of the overflow that belongs to you. "Well, just be grateful that

"God designed there would
be overflow. He was showing
us His nature. He not only
supplies our needs, but He's
an overflow God — a God
of more than enough."

Joel

you're getting by." Yes, we're grateful; but you don't have to stop there. "Lord, thank You that You're El Shaddai — the God of more than enough. Thank You that overflow is headed my way."

The Scripture says when you honor God, when you tithe your income, **God will open the windows of heaven and pour out a blessing that you cannot contain** (see Malachi 3:10). That's the overflow God; you can't contain it. Many of you have been faithful, you've given, served, helped others. Now God has some of these "cannot-contain blessings" coming your way.

One time in the Old Testament, the Israelites were in the desert, and they got tired of eating the manna. They came to Moses and said they wanted meat to eat. There were two million people out there. Moses said, "God, even if we butcher all of our flocks and all of our herds, we wouldn't have that much meat." God said, "Moses, when did I become weak? Have I lost my power? Don't you know I control the universe?" God shifted the winds and caused millions of quail to come into the camp. For miles everywhere they looked, quail were flying three feet off the ground. The Scripture says, "They gathered them up all day and all night and no one had less than fifty bushels of quail." Or you could say fifty boxes of steaks. One moment they were in lack, struggling, no sign of increase; the next moment they were in overflow — they had more than enough (see Numbers 11). What's interesting is that quail don't normally fly that far from the water. Normally they would never be out in the desert, but God shifted the winds, and suddenly the quail showed up.

A statistician ran some numbers based on the size of the Israelites camp and number of people, and quail three feet off the ground. He concluded that there were 105 million quail that came into the camp that day. God could have given them a couple quail each; that would have been four million quail. But God doesn't just want to supply your needs. He wants to give you overflow. He wants to bring you into more than enough.

A Testimony of God's Goodness

A friend of mine wanted to buy property to build a school on. He had some land but needed more. There were ten acres behind him connecting to his property. He had bought his land for $4,000 an acre. When he inquired about this new property, they wanted $25,000 an acre — more than five times what he paid for his. He didn't have the funds. He knew he was supposed to build this school, but he didn't see how it could happen. Instead of talking himself out of it, living discouraged, he kept thanking God that overflow was coming, and thanking Him that He was a more-than-enough God. Three years later, a man from the government unexpectedly came knocking on his door. He had never met this man, and he had never told him he was looking for property.

But this man told my friend that there were 120 acres right across the street that had nine buildings on it; the property had been foreclosed on five times. This man said, "I've been authorized to get rid of it; make me an offer, and we'll see what we can do." At $25,000 an acre, like the property behind him, the land alone would be $3 million; plus it had nine nice buildings on it that he could use for a school. My friend said, "I'll give you $200,000." The man shook his hand and said, "You have a deal." He got the nine

buildings and 120 acres for less than ten percent of its value.

You may not see how you could come into overflow — how you could have more than enough. But all God has to do is shift the winds, cause the right people to be good to you, cause that contract to come your way, cause that loved one you've never met to leave you an inheritance. All the circumstances may say it's impossible. God is asking you what He asked them, "When did I become weak? Is there any limit to my power?" Get in agreement with God. He's about to shift some things in your favor. He's about to open a door that no man can shut. He's about to put you at the right place at the right time. He's going to cause the quail to find you. He's going to make things happen that you didn't see coming. We look at our situations in the natural, but we serve a supernatural God. He has ways to increase you that you've never thought of. Just a shift here and suddenly you're in overflow — a shift there, and suddenly you have blessings that you cannot contain!

Faith Reflection

God is not limited by your job, by your salary, by what family you come from. He knows how to increase you. One good break, one idea, one inheritance, one contract can put you into more than enough. I'm asking you to get ready for overflow. Get ready for blessings that you cannot contain. "Joel, I don't see how this can happen." You don't have to see how. All you have to do is believe.

"God is about to do a new
thing. He has explosive
blessings — blessings that
catapult you to a new level.
One touch of His favor
will take you from having
just enough to having
more than enough!"

Joel

CHAPTER 11

PREPARING FOR NEW *Blessings*

"Let us keep looking to Jesus. Our faith comes from Him and He is the One Who makes it perfect. He did not give up when He had to suffer shame and die on a cross. He knew of the joy that would be His later. Now He is sitting at the right side of God."

Hebrews 12:2, NLV

God's way of getting us ready for new levels, getting us ready for more abundance might surprise you. In gardening terms, it's called pruning — cutting back a plant or a tree on purpose to prepare it for future growth. When we go through these seasons, it's good to know that God's pruning is not because you've done something wrong; it's not because God has forgotten about you. It's a test. Will you abide, will you stay in faith? Yes, the pruning is uncomfortable; we don't like it, but it's a part of the process. It's what leads to much fruit. You can't get too much or rise higher without being cut back. If you don't understand this, you'll get discouraged, "Why did this happen to me? I come to church every week. I volunteer at the hospital. I'm the one that always cheers people up; now I'm down." That's not the enemy trying to stop you; that's God getting you prepared for new levels. The apostle Paul never prayed for God to take away the difficulties. He asked God to give him the strength to endure whatever came his way.

If we could pray away the cutback seasons, then Jesus would have done it. The Scripture says in **Hebrews 12:2 that He endured the pain of the cross, looking forward to the joy that was coming.** Some things you have to endure. The way to do it is to know that it's not permanent, and to know that you're going to come out better. He endured the pain, looking forward to the joy that was coming. Keep reminding yourself that a cutback is leading to new growth. What's interesting is God cuts us back when we're bearing fruit—not when we're doing wrong or when we're off course, but when we're doing right, when things are going well.

Abide in Faith

The good news is God is the only One who can prune you. He's in control of the cutbacks. When Satan wanted to test Job, he couldn't go get the pruning shears and do whatever he wanted. He had to ask God for permission. When you get cut back, when you go through loss, things that don't make sense, remind yourself that God has the pruning shears. He knows exactly when and where to cut. He's not going to prune you to where you end up with less—less joy, less strength, less influence. That may temporarily happen. But if you'll keep abiding, then that cutback is making room for more fruit. God wouldn't have allowed it if He wasn't going to bring you out better, stronger, wiser, with new growth. You may be in a cutback season right now, wondering how you went from doing great to where you are. You were being your best, but It seems like you've lost ground. Yes, but the loss is only temporary. Stay in faith.

A while back, a cable network that aired our program on Sunday nights informed us that they were going to start running movies in that spot. They had to cancel our contract. We had been on that network for thirty-five years — way back with my father. We had a loyal audience, people that watched us faithfully. It was our only commercial airing on Sunday nights. At first, I was disappointed. I thought, "God, I don't want to go backward; I want to go forward." That was one of our best outlets. Here I was doing the right thing, we were bearing fruit, and people were being helped. Sometimes God closes doors that we don't understand. It doesn't make sense. I've been buying airtime for years, starting back with my father, and you can't buy time at night. It looked like that cutback was permanent.

About six months later, a man we worked with called and said, "Joel, I couldn't get another cable network on Sunday night, but I got the broadcast networks ABC, CBS, NBC, and they agreed to move their Sunday night programming after the news so they can air your program. The audience on those broadcast stations is three times what it was on that cable network. I went from fruit to more fruit. But notice the process: I was cut back. I didn't understand it. It didn't look like a good thing at the time, but now I say, "Lord, thank You for that cutback. Thank You for opening doors I never dreamed would open. Thank You for ordering my steps."

The cutback you're disappointed with now, if you'll keep abiding, keep thanking God, keep being your best, one day you'll look back and say like I did: "Lord, thank You. Your ways are better than my ways. You can see things I can't see." Trust Him in the cutback seasons. Believe that He's directing your steps. Remember, He has

"Believe that He's directing
your steps. Remember, He
has the pruning shears.
The enemy can't cut you
back. God has a hedge of
protection around you."

Joel

the pruning shears. The enemy can't cut you back. God has a hedge of protection around you.

God Knows What He's Doing

Steve Jobs was one of the most brilliant minds of our generation. He founded the company Apple and put his heart and soul into it. It grew bigger and bigger, and it became very successful. But over the years, he had conflict with his board; and eventually they voted him out. He was fired from the company that he started. That didn't seem fair. He could have sat around feeling sorry for himself, upset and bitter; instead, he went out and started another company. It was so successful that a few years later Apple bought his company and put him back in charge. He said, "If I had not been fired by Apple, I would have never learned these new skills that made me into who I am."

God knows what He's doing. He won't let you be cut back without a purpose. It may look like a bad break, but if you'll keep the right attitude, you'll see how it works out to your advantage. God knows when to prune; He knows when to take something away. It's not to hinder you but to promote you. If that person left you, it wasn't an accident. Their part in your story was over; God pruned them. If the project didn't last, it wasn't supposed to; God shut the door. Don't get discouraged. Don't sit around thinking, poor old me. You're being pruned so you can bear much fruit. Get ready for the new things God is about to do. Get ready for new levels of God's favor. Get ready for abundance.

God's Plans for You Are Good

In the Scripture, when Abraham took his son Isaac to the top of the mountain to sacrifice him, we think of Isaac as being a little boy. But most scholars believe he was in his late teens. The scripture says he carried a large pile of wood for the fire. He could have resisted lying on the altar, resisted letting his father tie him up. But I believe he was willing to go through with it because he knew the knife was in the right hands. He knew he could trust his father. When you understand the pruning shears are in God's hands, when you know His plans for you are for good, when you know He won't cut you back without a purpose — whatever He takes away temporarily is so He can bring you out with more fruit. Then like Isaac, you won't be frustrated in the cutback season. You won't get bitter and lose your faith and think, "God where are You? It's not fair, I'm uncomfortable, I was doing the right thing. Why did I go backward?" You trust your Father. You know He's in control of the cutbacks. He wouldn't take you backward if He wasn't going to bring you out with much fruit. I've found God's idea of "much" is much different than our idea.

I thought I was doing good, working behind the scenes all those years for my father and putting his ministry on television. I never dreamed one day I would be preaching and people would be watching all over the world. That was much fruit. But what took me from fruit to more fruit to much fruit were not the good times, not the times everything fell into place. It was the cutbacks, the things I didn't understand, the loss of my father. I was disappointed; nobody wants to lose a loved one. But in all those times that didn't make sense, I've learned I can trust the One who has the pruning shears. I know

the enemy can't cut me back, so I've done my best to just keep abiding, to keep being faithful even though I could be frustrated, to keep doing the right thing even though the wrong thing has happened, and to keep thanking God through the loss, through the disappointment, through the times that don't seem fair. If you'll keep abiding, it may not happen overnight, but at some point, you're going to come out of that cutback season and come into a growing season from not enough to more than enough.

Faith Reflection

If you or a loved one are in one of these cutback seasons, recognize that God is getting you in position for more fruit. He wouldn't have pruned you if He didn't have something better coming. Now do your part and keep abiding. Keep thanking Him, keep doing the right thing, keep an attitude of faith. If you'll do this, I believe and declare that loss is not permanent. New doors are about to open, new relationships are on the way, negative situations are about to turn around. Because you abide in Him, abundance is coming, healing is coming, breakthroughs are coming, new levels of your destiny, in Jesus' name!

"God knows what He's doing.
He won't let you be cut back
without a purpose. It may
look like a bad break, but if
you'll keep the right attitude,
you'll see how it works
out to your advantage."

Joel

CHAPTER 12

EXPECT GOD TO EXCEED YOUR
Expectations

"See, I am doing a new thing! Now it springs up;
do you not perceive it? I am making a way in the
wilderness and streams In the wasteland."

Isaiah 43:19, NIV

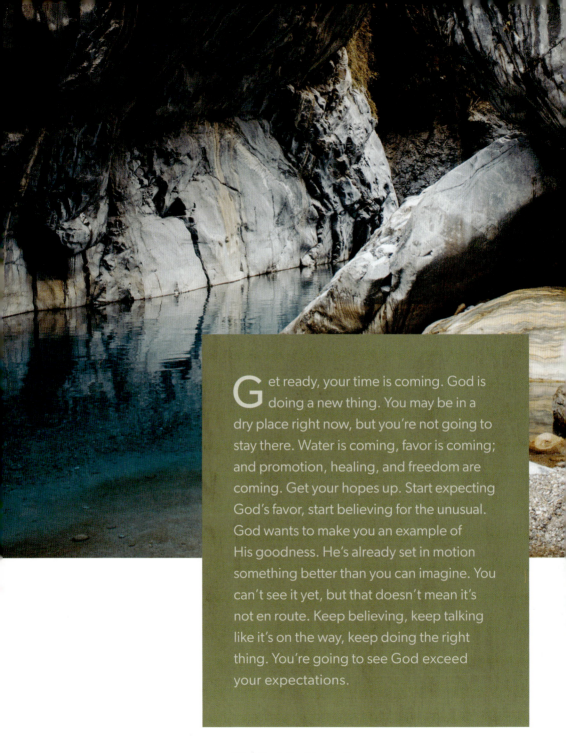

Get ready, your time is coming. God is doing a new thing. You may be in a dry place right now, but you're not going to stay there. Water is coming, favor is coming; and promotion, healing, and freedom are coming. Get your hopes up. Start expecting God's favor, start believing for the unusual. God wants to make you an example of His goodness. He's already set in motion something better than you can imagine. You can't see it yet, but that doesn't mean it's not en route. Keep believing, keep talking like it's on the way, keep doing the right thing. You're going to see God exceed your expectations.

A Mom's Dream Realized

I talked to a single mother living in Compton, California. There are a lot of great people in Compton but, of course, it's known for being a rough environment with gangs and drugs. Her husband was in the federal penitentiary. She's a schoolteacher; for thirteen years she raised her son by herself. There were a lot of negative influences and opportunities for him to get off course, but she's a praying mother. Even though she was in a dry place, she knew God could make streams in the desert. It seemed like they were held captive by their environment — a victim of their circumstances. Her son could have become a statistic, another child struggling, off course, on drugs; but she believed God was doing a new thing, that He was working behind the scenes. Every morning before school, they would listen to our messages, get the day started off in faith and hope and victory.

Her dream was for her son to go to college. All the odds were against him. She didn't have the funds. His father was in prison. His senior year, they applied to several different colleges and were waiting to hear back. One morning on their way to school, they heard me talking about how God has unprecedented favor, how He can make things happen that we can't make happen, how He wants to do a new thing. She heard that promise, and something came alive on the inside of her. She knew that was for them. Later that day, he received a handwritten letter in the mail. It said, "Congratulations, you've been accepted into Harvard University." He was the first African-American student ever accepted from Compton. During his senior year at Harvard, He was chosen as a Rhodes Scholar — one of only thirty-two from America. Not long ago, he was accepted into Yale Law School.

If you could see what God is doing behind the scenes in your life, you would be amazed. He's already lined up the good breaks, the right people, solutions to problems. The new thing is not going to be ordinary. It's going to catapult you ahead.

Let God Surprise You

The Scripture in Isaiah 43:19 (NIV) says, *"Do you not perceive it?"* It implies that God can be doing something but there's no sign of it. This mother could have thought nothing was happening for many years. When her son was thirteen, she didn't have the funds for college; fourteen, no funds; fifteen, nothing better. She was in the desert and didn't see any sign of rivers — no sign that things were going to change. But just because you don't see anything doesn't mean it's not on the way. At the right time, it's going to show up.

When God says He's going to do a new thing, that means it's not going to be like the old thing. It's going to be different. The new thing may not be what you were expecting. It may not happen the way you thought it would. The Israelites could have thought, "God, just defeat these Egyptians, and we'll live here." They didn't think God would take them into the desert. How could they survive out there? God was going to do it a different way. He was going to make streams in the desert. Stay open for how God is going to do it. Don't put Him in a box and limit Him to one way. Most of the time, the way we want it done is less than what God has in mind. What He has planned will be much bigger, much better. Trust Him to do it His way. If we're set on how we want it to happen, we can miss the new thing.

"Just because you don't see anything doesn't mean it's not on the way. At the right time, it's going to show up."

Joel

Keep Looking Ahead for God

A few years after I started ministering, the church began to grow. I thought we would build a new auditorium. That's the way I had seen my father do it growing up. He had built sanctuary after sanctuary. We found some property right off the freeway by the other location. It seemed perfect to me, but when we went to close on it, the owner sold it out from under us. He didn't keep his word. I was disappointed. I knew that property was supposed to be ours. We found another 100-acre tract not far away, and the same thing happened. I couldn't understand why these doors kept closing. There were no more large tracts of land to build on by the other location. My father always said that he would never move the church. My mind wasn't open for the new thing God had in store. About six months later, the Compaq Center became available. I never dreamed we could have this building. This was so much bigger, better than I ever imagined. It was a three-year battle, but we saw the hand of God make rivers in the desert, move giants out of the way, and bring the right people to help us.

We had a consultant that was very influential; he knew all the inner workings of the city. He had never been to church — didn't have anything to do with God or faith. He partied, used bad language, cursed people out. But He said, "Joel, I like you; and I'm going to help you get this building." God has already lined up the people you need for the new thing. Stay open. It may not happen the way you're expecting, but can I encourage you, God's way will be better, bigger, more rewarding, more fulfilling. Don't limit what you've seen in the past to what God is going to do in your future. God

never does His greatest feats in your yesterdays; they are always in your tomorrows.

God was saying in Isaiah, "I am the one that opened a way through the waters, making a dry path through the sea. I called forth the mighty armies of Pharaoh and drowned them in the waters. But forget about all of that; it's nothing compared to what I'm about to do. For I am doing a brand-new thing." This brand-new thing God is about to do is not going to be like anything you've seen in the past. We all can look back and see where God has parted the Red Sea in our lives . . . where He opened up a door that shouldn't have opened, had us in the right place at the right time. We got the job, we met that person and fell in love, He turned our health around when it didn't look good. We're grateful. We know it was the hand of God. But God is saying, "You haven't seen anything yet. Forget about all that and get ready for something awesome, something that you haven't seen, something that propels you to a new level." When you see this new thing, you're going to stand in amazement and say, "Wow, look what the Lord has done."

I believe the reason God told them to forget about the Red Sea being parted and forget about how He brought them out of slavery is because they would have thought He was going to do it the same way. After all, those were great miracles. But God was saying, "I have something better. Instead of parting the waters, I'm going to create the waters. I'm going to make rivers in the desert, pools to refresh you. I'm going to turn barren land into fertile land." The new thing God has for you is going to supersede what you've seen in the past. The good news is it's already in motion, the process has already

begun. Even now, it's springing forth. It's underground, behind the scenes; you can't see it, but the river is forming, the water is coming, the barren land is being fertilized. Yes, the doors may have closed, but don't worry! Your Compaq Center is already built, and the right people are already en route. The Red Sea parting was great, but it's nothing compared to what's coming.

Faith Reflection

Here's my question for you: Do you believe that God's up to something amazing, or are you looking back at what used to be, what didn't work out? Change your focus. No more looking in the rearview mirror! Start looking forward, start expecting His goodness. This is a new day. God is doing a new thing in your life. If you'll receive Isaiah's prophecy, I believe and declare you're about to see unusual favor, uncommon increase, rivers in your desert, water in the dry places. Like the Israelites, you'll be freed from captivity, lack, addictions, sicknesses. You're going to rise higher, overcome obstacles, and become all you were created to be. In Jesus' name.

"You could see your new thing tomorrow, you could see your breakthrough this week, you could get that scholarship this month; or you could see your healing, your promotion, your abundance this year!"

Joel

Giving the world HOPE through our media outreaches!

For a full listing, visit
JoelOsteen.com/How-To-Watch

BOOKS BY JOEL OSTEEN

Starting Your Best Life Now

You Can, You Will

Think Better, Live Better

The Power of I Am

Next Level Thinking

Every Day a Friday

Blessed in the Darkness

Peaceful on Purpose

You Are Stronger Than You Think

Stay in the Game

Your Greater Is Coming